FUN-TO-LEARN
SPORTS
FACTS FOR
CHILDREN

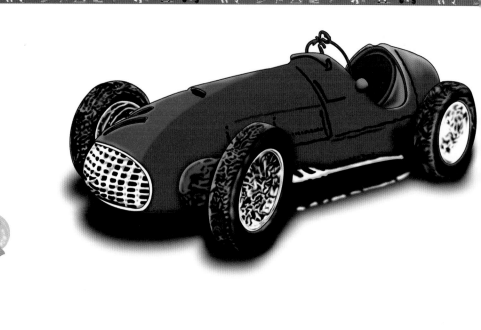

This edition published in 2004

Grandreams Books Ltd
4 North Parade, Bath BA1 1LF, UK

Designed & packaged by
Q2A Design Studio
Printed in China

Contents

Where and when did golf first originate?

Golf, a 15th century Scottish creation, was said to be influenced by the Roman game, pagancia, the Dutch game, Kolven and Belgian's Chole. However, these games did not include golf's most important feature - the hole.

When were the first official golf rules written?

The Gentleman Golfers of Leith, the world's first golf club, wrote the first 13 rules of golf in 1744.

In which year was golf accepted as a world sport?

Golf became internationally recognised when it was included in the 1900 Olympic Games.

What were some of the different names used for the game of golf?

The Scots called the game 'gowf,' the English called it 'goff,' while the Dutch referred to it as 'koff'.

What factors led to the growth of golf across the world?

The growth of industries, railways and tourism led to a rise in travel and leisure. More and more golf clubs were developed across Britain. Golf became more organised and competitive in the UK, followed by India and the USA.

What role did James VI of Scotland play in promoting golf?

James the VI, who later became King James I of England, found the game of golf appealing. His interest in golf led to a widespread acceptance of the sport in 17th century Great Britain.

Which was the earliest written reference to the game of golf?

The earliest written record of golf was in 1457. To fight off the English armies, Scotland's King James II needed well-trained archers. So, he ordered a ban on football and golf and encouraged the practice of archery instead.

Which Scottish golf course is known as the 'Home of Golf'?

Golf has been played on the Links at the St. Andrews Old Course since the 1400s. Regarded as the 'Home of Golf,' the course changed many times until it set the 18-hole standard. St Andrews Links is also Europe's largest golf complex and the world's oldest course.

Which was the first country to take up golf after Britain?

India was the first country after Great Britain to take up golf. The Royal Calcutta Golf Club of 1829 is the oldest golf club in India and the first outside of Great Britain.

Why is the Ladies' Golf Club at Scotland's St. Andrews a part of golf history?

This was the first club for women golfers. It was founded in 1867.

King James I

St. Andrews

What is the basic aim of golf?

The objective of the game is to drive a small ball into a hole with the fewest possible number of hits.

On which piece of equipment does the golf ball stand?

Golf balls are placed on the tee, a small peg stuck into the ground. Tees are usually made of wood or plastic and are used at the beginning of the game or at tee-off.

What is the Chili-Dip?

The Chili-Dip is a kind of golfing shot where the player hits behind the ball without moving it very far. The Chili-Dip is also known as a 'Fat Shot' or a 'Chunk.'

Caddie

How did the term 'caddie' come about?

A 'caddie,' or 'caddy,' is someone who carries a player's golf clubs during play and offers him help. The name was derived from Mary Queen of Scots helpers from the French Military, known in French as 'cadets.' Mary Queen of Scots introduced golf in France while she studied there.

In what way are scores recorded in golf?

Golf is the only sport where the scores are kept by fellow players and not by official scorekeepers. Players swap cards when a round begins, marking their own score as well as one another's.

What does 'ace' mean in a game of golf?

Ace is a hole-in-one made by golfers. It is a golfing score of 1 on any hole.

How is a golfer's swing defined?

Every swing taken at the ball is called a stroke and counts toward the golfer's total score. The player with the lowest score at the end of the game wins.

What is par?

Par is the number of strokes per hole it should take a player to put the ball in the cup, or the hole. It also means the expected total for the whole round of 18 holes.

Golfer's swing

How many golf clubs are players allowed to carry while putting?

Players are not allowed to have more than 14 clubs in their bags. If a player breaks a club during a round, they are allowed to fetch a new one, as long as it doesn't delay play.

Which rule allows the player to look for his lost golf ball?

A player can look for his lost ball, but according to the 5-Minute Rule, he has only 5 minutes to do so. If the ball is not found in that time, it is said to be lost and the player has to add a one-stroke penalty to his score.

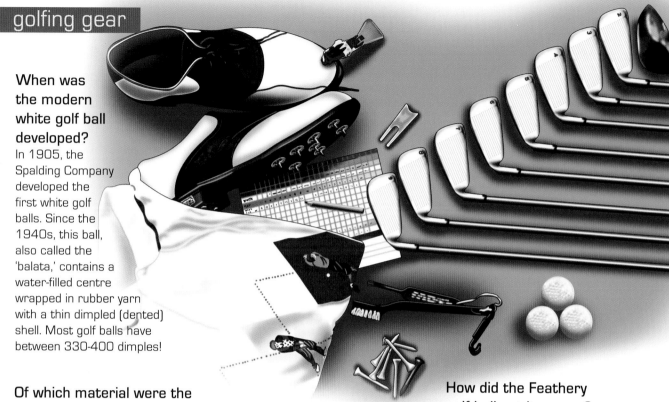

When was the modern white golf ball developed?

In 1905, the Spalding Company developed the first white golf balls. Since the 1940s, this ball, also called the 'balata,' contains a water-filled centre wrapped in rubber yarn with a thin dimpled (dented) shell. Most golf balls have between 330-400 dimples!

Of which material were the first-ever golf balls made?

The very first balls used in the game of golf were made of boxwood (the wood of the evergreen box tree).

What are the basic things needed to play golf?

A golf bag should consist of a set of 14 clubs, along with golf balls, tees, golf shoes and a scorecard. Some players also like to carry golf gloves.

Who made the earliest golf clubs?

The first creators of golf clubs were believed to be craftsmen who made bows and arrows for war. The first record found of such a craftsman was in 1603, when the court of James I of England hired William Mayne to make golf clubs for the king!

What did women wear when they played golf in the 1900s?

In the beginning, they wore blouses and long skirts. By 1910, golf was the only sport to allow women to wear tweed jackets with expanding pleats, which stopped clothes from tearing when the player swung at the ball.

What was the name of the first wound-up golf ball?

Coburn Haskell, an employee at Ohio's Goodrich and Tyre Rubber Company, made the first wound-up golf ball, the Haskell, in 1898. He felt that elastic thread wrapped around the inner rubber core of the golf ball would be superior to the gutty ball.

How did the Feathery golf ball get its name?

The Feathery ball, created in the 17th century, was much lighter than the earlier wood ball and could travel up to 200 yards. It was as light as a feather and so was named the Feathery.

From what material were early golf clubs made?

For around 200 years golf was played with wooden clubs, which were known as 'play clubs' and 'spoons.' The woods were slowly replaced with stronger iron, steel shaft and titanium clubs.

Which type of golf ball was made to replace the Feathery?

The Feathery was too costly for most people, so the gutta percha ball, or 'gutty,' was made in 1848. Gutta percha is a flexible material taken from Malaysian trees. It made the production of golf balls cheaper.

How is Arthur Pedrick linked to golf?

British inventor Arthur Pedrick designed a golf ball that could be steered while it was in the air! Pedrick patented as many as 162 inventions over 15 years, but none of them were marketed.

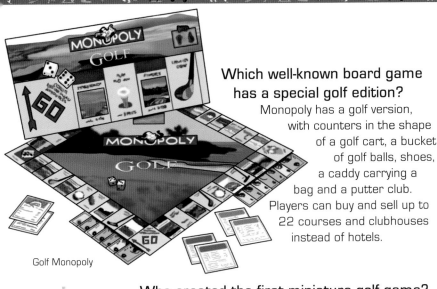

Golf Monopoly

Which well-known board game has a special golf edition?

Monopoly has a golf version, with counters in the shape of a golf cart, a bucket of golf balls, shoes, a caddy carrying a bag and a putter club. Players can buy and sell up to 22 courses and clubhouses instead of hotels.

What was Luther Simjian's contribution to the game of golf?

Turkish-born Luther George Simjian developed the first computerised indoor golf practice range in the 1960s. He used an analog computer to calculate and show the flight of the ball on a screen.

Who created the first miniature golf game?

Miniature golf, a putting game played on a small and artificial course, was first created by Garnet Carter, who licensed the miniature golf game, Tom Thumb Golf, in 1927.

Miniature golf

Which unusual golf tournament took place in France on Sundays?

The Calvin Klein Golf in Paris tournament was a two-round competition held in the parks and gardens of the French capital city. Players had to tee off from the city's bridges, tennis courts and even the foot of the Eiffel Tower!

What is Golden Tee Golf?

Golden Tee Golf is the most popular coin-operated video game in history. Created by Incredible Technologies in Chicago, it is available at over 50,000 bars and pubs in America.

Which modern game combines golf and football?

GolfCross, a game developed by New Zealand's Burton Silver, uses golf clubs to shoot rugby-shaped golf balls into netted goals! The same golf clubs, except the putter, are also used to hit the oval golf balls into nets suspended high in the air.

What is disc golf?

In disc golf flying golf discs are thrown at targets, instead of using clubs to hit a ball into a hole.

Why is the old sport of Jeu de Mail known as a type of golf?

Originally an Italian game, Jeu de Mail was taken up in Southern France in the early 17th century. The aim, as in traditional golf, was to hit a ball with a wooden club along a half-mile course to a fixed point. It later spread to England by the name of 'Pall Mall'.

Why is speed golf so called?

Speed golf is a variation of golf, in which the player runs while he or she shoots holes. In other words, speed golf, also called X-treme golf and fitness golf, combines the aim of golf with that of running.

Who invented the game of snow golf?

Indian-born writer Rudyard Kipling, who lived in Vermont, Canada in the 1890's, devised snow golf. He painted the golf balls red so that they could be seen in the snow!

Snow golf

Where is the world's longest golf course?

The International Golf Club in Massachusetts stretches a long par 77, 8325 yards from the tiger tees. It also boasts the world's largest hole - the 695 yard, 5th hole which is a par 6.

Why is the Gulmarg golf course special?

The Gulmarg green in Kashmir, India is the world's highest-situated golf course, at an altitude of almost 3000 metres (9,843 ft). It also has the longest golf hole in India.

Are there any golf courses in Walt Disney World?

Walt Disney World in Florida, USA has not one, but 5 courses and 1 nine-hole course. The Magnolia is the longest of these courses. Free yellow taxi vouchers are given to those resort guests who go to play golf at any of these courses.

What are archaic golf courses?

Archaic golf courses are those that are modelled to look like ancient courses. They have natural grass that is not trimmed. Oakhurst Links in West Virginia, USA, is one such course. It hosts a yearly champion-ship where contestants can only use hickory-shafted clubs and gutta percha balls.

Which movies were filmed at the Ocean Creek Golf Club?

This golf course in South Carolina, USA has been the site for many Hollywood movies. Scenes from Forrest Gump and Disney's Live Action Jungle Book were shot along these greens.

Where did former US President Bill Clinton go to play golf in May 2001?

The ex-US President flew by helicopter to the St. Andrews Royal and Ancient's Old Course, the 'Home of Golf.' He used a 50 year old guidebook to help him play the game!

Clinton playing golf

Where were the first American outdoor miniature golf courses?

The earliest outdoor miniature greens in the USA were built on rooftops in New York City, in 1926.

Where is the world's longest golf hole?

It is the 7th hole, par 7, of the Sano Course at the Satsuki Golf Club in Japan. It measures a shocking 909 yards!

What was found under the grounds of the Woburn Golf and Country Club in England?

While construction workers were digging the ground of this golf course in Buckinghamshire in 1999, they found mortar bombs containing mustard gas dating back to the Second World War.

Which golf course has America's oldest golf hole?

The first hole at The Homestead Golf Course in Michigan, USA is the oldest existing golf hole in America.

What are the different types of grass planted on golf greens?

Golf course surfaces are usually covered with bent grass (thin blades of grass for seasonal climates), froghair (tall, thick and difficult to play on), gorse (very thick grass), rough (high and coarse grass) or Bermuda grass (thick and grainy, found in warm places).

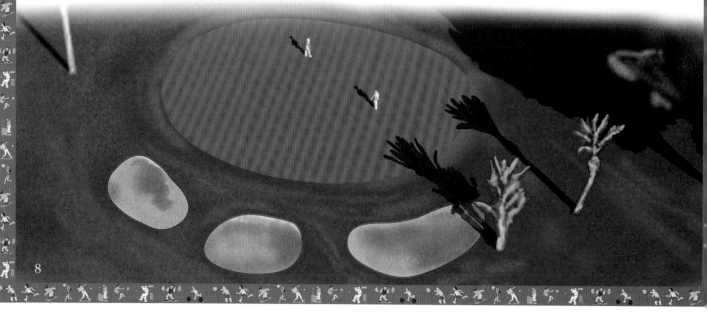

HOME

Which company was the first to sponsor a golf tournament?

In 1933 the Hershey Chocolate Company became the first corporate sponsor for the PGA TOUR, with the Hershey Open.

When did golf tournaments in the USA first become popular?

Tournament golf became popular as a spectator sport in the United States during the 1920s.

In which year did the British Open begin?

The British Open, the oldest of the major tournaments, began in 1860 to find the champion golfer of the world. Only professional golfers competed in the first tournament but, later, amateurs were also allowed to participate.

What kind of golf tournament is held in Greenland every year?

At the annual Drambuie World Ice Golf Championships, held near the Arctic Circle, 36 golfers compete on a course made up of glaciers and icebergs. Temperatures can fall down to -50°C. The golf ball used is fluorescent orange, to enable it to be seen in the white snow!

In which year was the earliest recorded women's golf tournament held?

The first game of golf for women took place in 1810, in Musselburgh, Scotland. In 1897, the first-ever women's golf club was also opened at St. Andrews, Scotland.

Ryder Cup

What did the trophy of the first Open Championship look like?

The winner of the first Open Championship, played at Prestwick, Scotland, in 1860, was awarded with a wide belt of rich red morocco leather, decorated with silver buckles and emblems.

At what time does the annual Canadian North Yellowknife Midnight Golf Classic begin?

This tournament, held at Canada's all-sand Yellowknife Golf Course each June 21st weekend, tees off at midnight and finishes at about six o'clock the next morning. It was originally called the Midnight Marathon in 1948.

When was the first Ryder Cup Tournament held?

Ryder Cup matches were first held in 1927 and the tournament was won by the USA.

Where and when was the first Canada Cup tournament held?

The first Canada Cup golf tournament was held in 1953 at the Beaconfield Golf Club in Montreal, in which 7 countries participated. In 1967, the Canada Cup changed its name to the World Cup.

What piece of clothing is awarded to winners of the Masters?

Winners of the Masters are presented with the Green Jacket, one of the greatest prizes in sport. The first Green Jacket was awarded to golfer Sam Snead in 1949.

Tiger Woods wearing the Green Jacket

Bernhard Langer

Which unusual record does Bernhard Langer hold?

Bernhard Langer is the only player to have climbed an oak tree in search of his golf ball two times in his career!

What is the meaning of golfer Vijay Singh's first name?

He is Fiji's only world-class golfer and his first name means 'victory' in the Indian language of Hindi. Vijay Singh learnt golf from his father, who was an aeroplane technician.

Jack Nicklaus

What nickname has been given to golfing legend Jack Nicklaus?

This American golfer became popularly known as the 'Golden Bear' because of his blond hair! Jack Nicklaus was the first player in history to win all four golf major titles at least twice. He has also designed many golf courses.

What was unusual about a shot played by Leonard Crawley at the 1932 Walker Cup?

At this tournament, famous golfer Leonard Crawley's shot into the 18th green hit the actual Walker Cup trophy, putting a dent into it.

Why is Gary Player called the 'Black Knight'?

This South African player is commonly known as 'Black Knight' because of his habit of wearing black on the golf course.

Who is the youngest male golfer to qualify for a professional golf match?

Thirteen-year-old Korean player Jae An is the youngest male to qualify for a men's pro tournament.

Why is Mildred 'Babe' Didrikson Zaharias one of the greatest women golfers of all time?

Mildred 'Babe' Didrikson Zaharias only took up golf after retiring from an athletics career, during which she won 3 Olympics gold medals and broke several world records. She won 55 golf tournaments, including 17 in a row in 1947. She also became the first American to win the 1947 British Women's Amateur championship.

At what age did Tiger Woods first play golf?

Tiger Woods, whose real name is Eldrick Woods, started playing golf when he was just nine months old!

Who was the first golfer to market equipment with his name on it?

Walter Hagen was the first to have his own line of golf gear. It is believed he once played golf in a tuxedo to annoy his fellow partner.

What kind of food does Tiger Woods eat to win tournaments?

In his first published book, 'How I Play Golf,' Tiger Woods talks about the foods that he believes are lucky for him, like turkey, baked fish, skimmed milk, egg whites and rice. He never takes pizza, ice cream, roast beef, fried chicken, gravy, crisps, ham or soft drinks before a game.

Tiger Woods

Which golfer won the maximum tournaments in women's golf history?

American golfer Patty Berg (Patricia Jane Berg) achieved this record. During 1935-1964, she won 83 tournaments. Berg was also the first president of the Ladies Professional Golf Association (LPGA). In 1946, she won the first ever U.S. Women's Open.

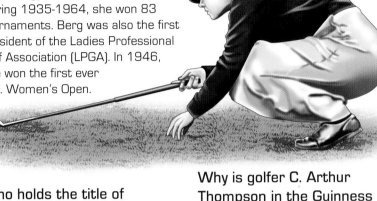

Patty Berg

Who is the only sportsman to have won four major titles in just one year?

Bobby Jones (Robert Tyre Jones) won the US Open, the British Open, the United States Amateur and the British Amateur tournaments in 1930. Today, Bobby Jones is the brand name for the Hickey-Freeman Company's collection of golf clothes.

Bobby Jones

Who holds the title of the youngest golfer to become No.1?

As a 21-year-old, Tiger Woods became the youngest-ever number one golfer in the world. He broke the earlier record of Germany's Bernhard Langer, who was 29 when he reached this position.

Why is golfer C. Arthur Thompson in the Guinness Book of Records?

C. Arthur Thompson is in the Guinness Book of World Records for being the oldest player ever to score as much as, or less than, his age in an 18-hole round. In 1973, at the age of 103, Thompson scored exactly 103!

Which golfing championship game had a record number of participants?

At the 1984 Volkswagen Grand Prix Open Amateur Championship in the UK, the number of competitors reached a record 321,779. These included 206,820 men and 114,959 women.

Who stacked a pile of golf balls on top of each other without adhesive?

In October 1998, Don Athey from Ohio, USA piled up nine golf balls vertically, without any glue!

Who took two years to make a single golf tee?

Des Sawa Jr. from Ontario, Canada made a golf tee 2.2 metres (7.2ft) long, from a 130-year-old maple wood tree in September 1999.

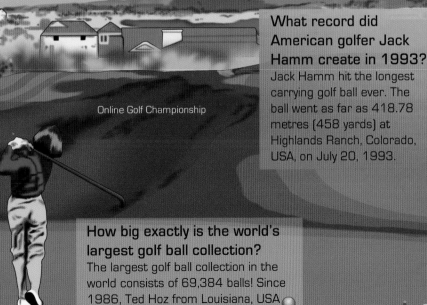

Online Golf Championship

What record did American golfer Jack Hamm create in 1993?

Jack Hamm hit the longest carrying golf ball ever. The ball went as far as 418.78 metres (458 yards) at Highlands Ranch, Colorado, USA, on July 20, 1993.

For which tournament did over 11,000 players sign up?

Over 11,000 players enrolled for the largest Internet golf game. The 1999 Jack Nicklaus Online Golf Championships were won by USA's Chet Stone after putting 36 holes on the digitised Pelican Hill course in California.

How big exactly is the world's largest golf ball collection?

The largest golf ball collection in the world consists of 69,384 balls! Since 1986, Ted Hoz from Louisiana, USA has been adding to this collection, which if arranged in a line, would extend almost 2 miles (3.2 km)!

What did Lori Garbacz do to protest against the slow pace of play at a golf tournament?

The first two rounds of the 1999 US Women's Open were so slow that golfer Lori Garbacz ordered a Dominoes pizza while waiting her turn!

GolfCross ball

What did Burton Silver invent?

In 1989 inventor, cartoonist and writer Burton Silver from New Zealand created an oval golf ball. The rugby football-shaped golf ball, which took 12 years to make, was made for GolfCross, a type of golf game that's played with net goals rather than holes!

When was the golf term 'birdie' coined?

'Birdie,' a golf score, was first so called by Ab Smith at the Atlantic City Country Club in 1898, when he said to another, "that was a 'bird of a hole'."

How is astronaut Alan Shepherd linked to the game of golf?

Alan Shepherd, the first American to fly in space and one of 12 men to walk on the moon, was also the only person ever to play golf on the moon! It is believed that the ball was not found again. The club he used can be seen at the United States Golf Association (USGA) museum.

In which James Bond movie did Agent 007 play golf for the first time?

In the 1964 film 'Goldfinger' starring Sean Connery, secret agent James Bond played golf for the first time!

Why did disabled golfer Casey Martin file a case against PGA Tour authorities?

In 1997, he filed a case against PGA officials, who were not allowing him to ride a golf cart in competitions. In 2001, the U.S. Supreme Court permitted him to use an electric cart in pro tournaments.

Why was businessman Robert Barcock sent to jail?

This 48-year-old was sentenced to 30 months in prison after thousands of Spalding golf balls, worth £150,000, were found at his warehouse. The police found 9,757 boxes, each containing 18 balls, at his store house in October 2001. He was found guilty of stealing the balls.

Which is the oldest published golf magazine in the USA?

The Professional Golfer of America is the oldest golf magazine in the USA to be continuously published since 1920. It is today known as the PGA Magazine.

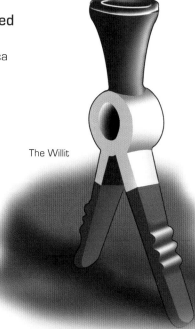

The Willit

Where did the popular golf word 'fore' come from?

'Fore' is a warning call shouted out to anyone in danger of being struck by a golf ball. The word is short for 'ware before,' a wartime command for the first line of shooters to kneel down for the second line to fire.

What is the Willit?

The Willit is a two-pronged golf tee inspired by a visit to the dentist! Millionaire inventor Dr. William Johnson got his idea from a poster at his dentist's, that showed how teeth with two roots are held in the gums.

St. Andrews
Starter's Box

OLD
COURSE
STARTER

What object at the St. Andrews golf course was sold as an antique?

The antique starter's box, from which instructions were given to players, was sold for £59,000 to an American golfer. Celebrities like Bill Clinton, Michael Douglas, Sean Connery and Jack Nicholson have passed through this box.

Freddie Tait

Which South African museum is named after a Scottish golfer?

The Freddie Tait Golf Museum, the first of its kind in South Africa, is named after the famous Scottish player, Freddie Tait, who died during the Battle of Koodoosberg in 1890.

Where is the world's largest collection of old golf memorabilia?

The Canadian Golf Museum and Historical Institute has the world's largest set of vintage golf collectibles, including the earliest colour golf illustration and the club used by astronaut Alan Shepherd on the moon.

Where can one find the original golf shoes of President George Herbert Bush?

The former American President's golf shoes are at Germany's Weißenfels shoe museum. The US Ambassador's wife in Leipzig got the shoes from the President for the museum.

Where can one of the most famous golf paintings be seen?

The Golfers, painted in 1847 by Charles Lees, is at the Scottish National Portrait Gallery and is regularly exhibited at the British Golf Museum in St Andrews. The painting shows an historical Grand Match played over the Links of St Andrews.

What is the HumVee?

The HumVee is a collectible golf cart that was first sold in 1992. It is a version of the High Mobility Multipurpose Wheeled Vehicle or HMMWV.

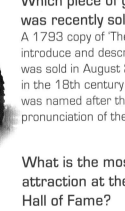

HumVee
golf cart

Which piece of golf memorabilia was recently sold at an auction?

A 1793 copy of 'The Goff,' the first book to introduce and describe the game of golf, was sold in August 2002. First published in the 18th century in Scotland, 'The Goff' was named after the old English pronunciation of the game.

Why is the Blanchard's Antique Golf and Sporting Museum unusual?

The Blanchard's Antique Golf and Sporting Museum in USA is the only museum in Alabama built out of a tobacco warehouse in 1909, ousing over 9000 golf clubs!

At which museum can you see a golf-themed toilet seat?

At the British Golf Museum in Scotland, the 21st century Golf Gallery features strange objects, including a golf-based toilet seat!

What is the most popular attraction at the PGA Golf Hall of Fame?

The PGA Golf Hall of Fame in the USA houses a 90 foot (27.4 metre) long display of original artwork, feather balls and vintage clubs to illustrate the complete history of golf. There is also a golf ball wall covered with over 13,000 logo balls.

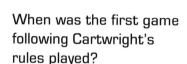

Logo - Cincinnati Reds

Where was baseball invented?

Nobody knows exactly when baseball was invented, but it was based on the children's English game, rounders. Different types of the game became popular in the USA in the early 19th century.

Who wrote the first official rules of baseball?

Alexander Joy Cartwright (1820-1892) of New York, USA wrote down the first official set of 20 baseball rules on September 23, 1845. He also invented the modern baseball field in the same year.

When were baseball uniforms worn for the first time?

The Knickerbockers of New York, USA, introduced baseball uniforms for the first time in 1849. Their uniforms had white flannel shirts, blue woollen pantaloons and straw hats!

'Babe' Ruth

When was the first game following Cartwright's rules played?

On June 19, 1846 at Elysian Field, New Jersey. The New York Nine beat the Knickerbockers 23-1. The Knickerbockers was Cartwright's own team!

When was the catcher's mask invented?

In 1877, Fred Thayer, captain of the Harvard University Baseball team invented it. He replaced the grill of traditional fencing with strong wire and a padded chin-piece. Harvard's catcher, Alexander Tyng, first wore the mask.

Why was baseball first known as Town Ball?

Rules of the game often varied from town to town, so the local form of baseball was called 'Town Ball'.

Who introduced the idea of the knob at the end of baseball bats?

Legendary baseball player 'Babe' Ruth. He ordered such a bat made, to keep it from slipping out of his hands when he swung it.

When were batting averages recorded for the first time in the history of baseball?

The first batting averages were recorded in 1871, starting with Boston and Cleveland.

Which team is considered baseball's first professional team?

The Cincinnati Red Stockings Club were the first to pay their players and so are known as the first professional baseball team. They won 72 games in a row.

Baseball catcher wearing his mask

Who was Henry Chadwick (1824-1908)?

He was the 'Father of Baseball.' Chadwick was a famous press reporter who made baseball popular by writing about it. He not only wrote the first hardcover book on baseball, 'The Game of Base Ball,' but also invented the modern box score and the batting average concept.

What does the term 'bases loaded' mean?

When the batting team has runners on the first, second and third bases, it is seen as a big chance for a grand slam and as a situation where the 'bases are loaded', 'juiced' or as having 'ducks on the pond'.

Who is known as a 'base coach'?

A coach who stands near the first or the third base. He instructs the batter and base runners about what to do with special hand signals.

Baseball coach

How did the term bullpen originate?

Nobody knows for sure, but it is believed that it came from the Bull Durham Red Tobacco advertisements, along the walls of the 'bullpens' themselves. Bullpens are the warm up areas on the field for pitchers, consisting of 2 mounds and 2 home plates.

In baseball, what is known as a 'grand slam'?

A grand slam is when a batter hits a home run when there are runners on every base. Because the ball is out of the grounds, they all cross the home plate, scoring 1 run each. So the batter's single home run actually gains the team 4 runs!

Base

Why are the bases used in baseball known as bags?

During the early years of baseball, teams would often use sacks filled with sand to mark base locations. That is why even today, bases are sometimes called 'bags'.

What kind of pitch is a 'change-up'?

A change-up is a slow pitch thrown with the exact arm action as a fastball. Pitchers use it to confuse the batter's timing.

What is a 'brushback'?

A brushback is a pitch that nearly hits the batter. It is also known as throwing 'high and tight'.

What kind of bat-grip is known as a 'choke-up'?

When the bat is gripped high on the handle, with both hands far from the knob.

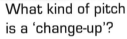

Bunt

What is the significance of 'The Curse of the Bambino'?

In 1920, Red Sox owner Harry Frazee sold Babe Ruth's (Bambino's) contract to the New York Yankees for $100,000. Since then, the Boston Red Sox have never won the World Series. It is believed that the team fell under Bambino's Curse after Babe Ruth left.

When does a batter 'bunt' the ball?

When the batter holds the bat still (does not swing to hit the ball) and lets the ball hit the bat. Batters use the bunt shot to surprise fielders or to help other runners to take a quick run.

How did the Louisville Slugger baseball bat originate?

At an 1884 Louisville game, woodworker John Hillerich saw Pete Browning break his favourite bat and offered to make him a new one, which soon became known as the Louisville Slugger. Honus Wagner was the first player to have his autograph burnt into this bat.

In which year was the first metal baseball bat licensed?

Metal bats were licensed to William Shroyer in 1924, but they were not seen in the game until 1970, when Worth introduced the first aluminum baseball bat.

Whose shoes are displayed at the National Baseball Hall of Fame and Museum?

Joseph Jefferson Jackson's shoes, which he took off during a 1908 game because of blisters on his feet. A fan saw this and shouted "Shoeless son of a gun!" Since then, Jackson was nicknamed 'Shoeless' Joe Jackson!

How did maple wood baseball bats become popular?

During a single baseball season in 2001, Barry Bonds set a record with 73 home runs. It was then revealed that Bonds used maple wood baseball bats, instead of the common white ash bats.

When was the earliest reference to the use of a baseball glove made?

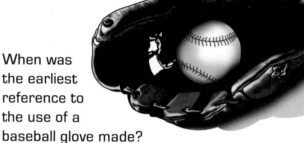

The first use of a baseball glove is believed to have been in June 1870. A sports journalist from the Cincinnati Commercial reported that Doug Allison caught balls with a pair of buckskin mittens during a match.

What did the 'Chicago Style' baseball cap look like?

This cap, made in the 1870s, was in the style of a pillbox (a small round hat worn by women) and had a flat top and horizontal stripes that made it look like layered cake!

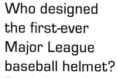

Is there a baseball that can time its own speed?

The Radar Ball is the world's first baseball that can time itself. Its built-in microchip calculates its travelling time from the pitcher to the home base, converts this into miles per hour and then displays the result on the LCD screen on its side. To reset the timer, the ball has to be tapped three times!

What is unique about the Copperhead ACX baseball bat?

This is the world's first electronic baseball bat, manufactured in 1998 by USA's ACX and Worth companies. Using technology developed for jet fighters, the bat is designed to reduce the 'sting' caused by vibrations from the collision between bat and ball. It costs $299.

Which set of historic baseball gear set a new auction record in 1999?

The Yankees uniform worn by baseball's original 'Iron Man', Lou Gehrig, on July 4, 1939, when he played his last professional match before retiring. An American bought the uniform for $451,541, a new record for auctioned uniforms.

Who designed the first-ever Major League baseball helmet?

Baseball legend Branch Rickey, inventor Ralph Davia and designer Ed Crick introduced the helmet in 1952 to encourage safety. Made of solid fibreglass, the helmet was fabric-coated to look like a cloth cap.

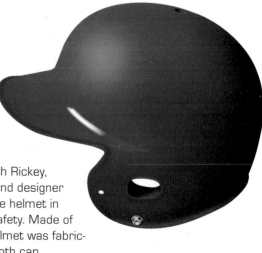

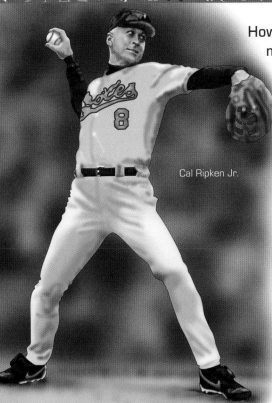

Cal Ripken Jr.

How many Major League matches in succession did Cal Ripken Jr. complete in 1995?

In September 1995, he broke Lou Gehrig's 56-year-old record with his 2,131st consecutive game. Calvin Edwin Ripken Jr. is also known as baseball's 'Iron Man', after Lou Gehrig.

Which umpire served the most Major League seasons?

William Klem from America umpired matches for 37 years during 1905-1941. Klem also invented arm signals to go with his calls.

When was the concept of Major League baseball born?

Major League baseball was established with the origins of the National League, in 1876 and the American League, in 1900. The two Leagues expanded and joined up to represent Major League baseball in the 1960s.

Why is William Mays' 1954 catch famous?

In September 1954, at the New York Polo Grounds, USA, Willie Mays ran full speed after Vic Wertz hit a ball that travelled 120 metres. He caught it over his left shoulder with his back to his base. This feat is popularly called 'The Catch'.

Which player appeared in only one Major League game?

In 1951, a midget by the name of Eddie Gaedel popped out of a 213 centimetre (7 ft) cake to play for the St. Louis Browns against the Detroit Tigers. He lasted in the game for just 2 minutes!

Who pitched the first-ever perfect Major League baseball game?

Boston's Denton True 'Cy' Young. Nobody from the other team could reach first base. Young was nicknamed 'Cy' because he was 'as fast as a cyclone'.

What are some of the popular Major League baseball team mascots called?

There is the furry green Phanatic of the Philadelphia Phillies, the San Diego Chicken of the Padres, Lou Seal of the San Francisco Giants, Fred the Bird of the St. Louis Cardinals, and Homer of the Atlanta Braves.

Fred the Bird

Which famous personality used to be a managing partner for the Texas Rangers?

George Bush

Before becoming President of the United States and Governor of Texas, President Bush was a managing partner for this Major League baseball team.

Who was the first live action mascot in Major League baseball?

In 1964, the 1.86 metres (6 ft 10 inch) tall Mr. Met, who first appeared as a cartoon, became the first live-action mascot for MLB's New York Mets team. Mr. Met wore the team uniform and sported a huge baseball head!

Which team has won the maximum number of Major League matches?

The 1998 New York Yankees have had no less than 125 victories.

17

Who were Eddie & Johnny O'Brien and Ozzie & Jose Canseco?

They were the only pair of twins to play on the same team in the entire history of the Major League!

O'Brian Twins

What gives Jackie Robinson a place in the history of baseball?

He was the first black baseball player to be inducted into the Baseball Hall of Fame. His Hall of Fame plaque was unveiled on July 23, 1962.

Jackie Robinson

Who was the first pitcher awarded with 4 Cy Young Awards?

Left-handed baseball pitcher Steve Norman Carlton won Cy Young Awards in 1972, 1977, 1980 and 1982.

Who was the first female to umpire a professional baseball game?

On June 24, 1972, Bernice Gera became the first woman to umpire a professional game - a New York-Pennsylvania League doubleheader.

How did George Ruth Jr. gain the nickname 'Babe'?

When Jack Dunn, the Baltimore Orioles manager and George Ruth Jr.'s legal guardian, took Ruth to the playing field, another player remarked, "Well, here's Jack's newest babe". The name stuck and George Ruth has since then been called Babe Ruth.

What do baseball players Hank Aaron, Willie Mays and Eddie Murray have in common?

They are the only three members of the 3,000 Hits Club who are also members of the 500 Home Runs Club!

What made baseball player Moses Fleetwood Walker special?

On 5th January 1884 he became the first-ever black baseball player to play in the Major League.

Who hit the first ever home run in Major League history?

Ross Barnes of the Chicago White Stockings, against the Cincinnati Red Stockings, in 1876.

Alex Rodriguez

What do Jose Canseco, Alex Rodriguez and Barry Bonds have in common?

They are the only players to have hit 40 home runs and stolen 40 bases, all during the same season!

Why are Matty and Felipe Alou especially remembered?

In 1996, Matty Alou of the Pittsburgh Pirates won the National League batting title with a 0.342 average. The runner-up was his brother Felipe. This was the first time that brothers finished 1st and 2nd in a batting race.

Which baseball pitcher recently became the richest contract-holder?

In December 2000, Mike Hampton of the LH Hamptons was given the richest contract ever for a pitcher, an eight-year, $121 million deal with the Colorado Rockies.

Mike Hampton

Which player has played the maximum number of Major League games during his career?

The legendary Pete Rose. During a 23-year long career, he played 3,562 Major League games. He also holds the Major League Record for most career hits - 4,256!

Mike Schmidt

Who holds the record for the longest home run in a Major League game?

In a September 1960 game against the Detroit Tigers, Mickey Mantle of the New York Yankees hit the ball 192.3 metres (634 feet) from the home plate.

What is the longest baseball throw on record?

Canadian Glen Gorbous threw a baseball that travelled 135.88 metres (445 ft and 10 inches) on August 1, 1957.

What is the name of the first baseball movie?

The Ball Game, the first-ever baseball film, was made in 1898 by Thomas Edison. It was about two amateur baseball teams from New Jersey, USA.

What record is held jointly by Mike Cameron, Rocky Colavito, Lou Gehrig, Bobby Lowe and Mike Schmidt?

Each of them hit 4 home runs during a single game!

Who holds the record for the fastest pitch?

Lynn Nolan Ryan of the California Angels. On August 20, 1974, in the Anaheim Stadium, he pitched the ball at 162.3 kilometres (100.9 miles) per hour.

Who holds the record for hitting a home run in the most number of consecutive National League games?

Dale Long of Pittsburgh. He hit a home run in 8 consecutive National League games!

Who holds the record for the fastest run around the bases?

Ernest Swanson. In 1932, in Ohio, USA, he ran around the bases in just 13.3 seconds, with an average speed of 29.70 kilometres (18.45 miles) per hour.

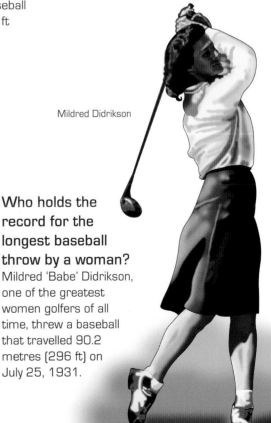

Mildred Didrikson

Who holds the record for the longest baseball throw by a woman?

Mildred 'Babe' Didrikson, one of the greatest women golfers of all time, threw a baseball that travelled 90.2 metres (296 ft) on July 25, 1931.

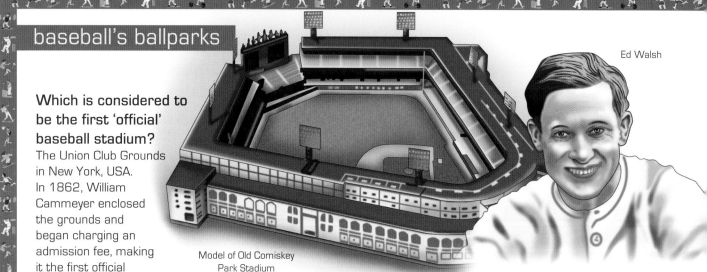

Ed Walsh

Model of Old Comiskey Park Stadium

Which is considered to be the first 'official' baseball stadium?

The Union Club Grounds in New York, USA. In 1862, William Cammeyer enclosed the grounds and began charging an admission fee, making it the first official baseball 'stadium'.

What kind of promotion activities did the Atlanta-Fulton County Stadium launch?

There was a Wedlock and Headlock Day where 34 couples were married before a Braves Vs Mets game and a wrestling match after it! The '$25,000 Cash Scramble', event gave fans a chance to grab as many single bills of this amount scattered across the field as they could in 90 seconds!

Where was the first-ever night game played?

At the Crosley Field ballpark in Ohio, USA. President Roosevelt switched on the lights by pushing a button from 500 miles away!

What unusual prize was offered to batters at the Ebbets Field Ballpark?

An 'Abe Stark' (a famous clothes store) advertisement was placed along one side. Any batter that hit the sign immediately won a free suit!

Which stadium was built with inputs from the National Baseball Hall of Fame pitcher, Ed Walsh?

Old Comiskey Park in Illinois, USA.

What occupied the site of the Bennett Park before the stadium was built?

Before Bennett Park ballpark existed, it was an old hay market where farmers brought their hay to be weighed and sold. Charlie Bennett, the Detroit Wolverines' catcher, threw the first pitch here for 31 years in a row!

Why did the Braves Field ballpark management have to pay $6,000 in legal claims to its fans?

This ballpark in Massachusetts, USA, did not warn fans about wet paint on the stadium seats. Over 50,000 fans left the stadium with green paint on their clothes!

Atlanta-Fulton County Stadium

Why was the Atlanta-Fulton County Stadium nicknamed 'The Launching Pad'?

Because an unusually high number of home runs were hit in this stadium.

What makes the Atlanta-Fulton County Stadium special?

Outside the stadium are three bronze statues honouring the legendary players Hank Aaron, Ty Cobb and Phil Niekro!

What was the New Comiskey Park stadium originally known as?

Charles Comiskey had first named the ballpark the 'Baseball Palace of the World'.

What is special about the Comerica Ballpark?

Comerica Park, home to the Tigers team, has a roundabout with hand-painted tigers and chariots to ride on. It also features a 50-foot giant wheel that has cars in the shape of baseballs and a fountain that changes colour and 'dances' to music to celebrate home runs!

What was the Buhner Buzz Cut Night?

Named after the Mariner's half-bald outfielder, Jay Buhner, this event gave free admission to fans who were bald or who got haircuts like Jay Buhner! They would also get free T-shirts saying 'Take me out to the Bald game' or 'Bald is Buhnerful'.

Which baseball fan came to ballparks with a frying pan and ladle?

Hilda Chester, considered the most famous baseball fan, attended games with a frying pan and an iron ladle. She would bang them together to cheer for her favourite team, the Dodgers, as she was not allowed to shout because of a heart problem!

Yankee Stadium

Which popular food item was launched at baseball arenas in 1893?

The hot dog was introduced as a main food attraction at baseball stadiums. It is believed that Chris von de Ahe, the St. Louis Brown team's owner, began the tradition of serving hotdogs at baseball games.

By what nickname is the Tokyo Dome known?

Tokyo Dome, Japan's first dome-shaped indoor baseball stadium, is known as the 'Big Egg'. It was built in March 1998.

What kind of a record does the Griffith Stadium hold?

The legendary Mickey Mantle hit the only home run that cleared this stadium in Washington DC, USA, hitting a 17.06 metres (56 ft) tall National Bohemian beer bottle sign standing outside!

For what reason is the first game at the Yankee Stadium specially remembered?

The legendary Babe Ruth hit a home run during the very first game played in this stadium in New York, USA.

Which baseball park in USA was the first to give fans Internet access?

The PacBell Park in San Francisco, California was the first Major League stadium in the country to have booths with Star Trek-type computers for limited but free Internet access.

In what way did the US Postal Service honour old ballparks in 2001?

The official postal service brought out a set of stamps featuring 11 famous old ballparks. The stamp collection, called 'Baseball's Legendary Playing Fields', includes Ebbet's Field, Forbes Field, Shibe Park, Comiskey Park, Wrigley Field, Crosley Field and the Polo Grounds.

Where is the Coca-Cola Superslide?

The Coca-Cola Superslide is a 24.38 metres (80 ft) long and 7.62 metres (25ft) wide model of a Coca-Cola bottle at the Pacific Bell Park in San Francisco, USA. It has many slides inside it and when a home run is hit, lights are flashed from it and bubbles float from its mouth!

Honus Wagner Card

Why did Atlanta Braves pitcher Pascual Perez miss starting a game against the Braves in August 1982?

Because he got lost! He went round the Interstate 285 twice, trying to find the exit that led to the Fulton County Stadium.

Why was St. Louis player George Toporcer known by the nickname 'Specs' Toporcer?

In 1921, infielder George Toporcer became the first non-pitcher to wear glasses at the field in a Major League game.

Which was the most expensive baseball card ever sold?

The T206 Honus Wagner card, one of the rarest and most sought-after baseball cards in the world, was sold on E-bay for $1.265 million!

Which famous US President was known to have played an early version of baseball?

George Washington. There is a record of a letter written by a soldier that describes Washington playing rounders with his soldiers at an army camp!

Which is the most expensive baseball artefact ever sold?

The ball with which Mark McGwire of the St. Louis Cardinals hit his 70th home run. It sold at an auction for $3 million! A normal baseball usually costs about $5 to make.

Why is the T206 Honus Wagner card so rare?

In the early 1900s, Honus Wagner insisted that the American Tobacco Company, who made the card, stop using his name to promote smoking. The company stopped making the cards, but about 50 to 60 were secretly distributed.

Which famous piece of baseball memorabilia is known as 'Black Betsy'?

Legendary baseball player 'Shoeless' Joe Jackson's baseball bat, which sold for $ 577,610 in an auction in 2001.

Why did Seattle player Rey Quinones once miss a call to come up to bat?

He'd gone back to the clubhouse to play Nintendo!

When were umpires paid for their services for the first time?

In 1878, the National League of Professional Baseball Clubs ruled that umpires should be paid for their services. They were paid $5 per game.

How much do baseball umpires earn nowadays?

Currently, Major League baseball umpires have contracts that are worth between $84,000 and $300,000 a year!

Umpire in action

What is the 3,000 Hits Club and who started it?

The 3,000 Hits Club was started by Cap Anson for batsmen who had scored 3,000 runs or above during their professional careers.

Which US President managed a baseball team for a short period of time?

In 1900, Franklin Roosevelt managed a baseball team called the Grotons!

How did Babe Ruth keep his head cool?

He used to put a cabbage leaf under his baseball cap and after every two innings, he would change the old leaf for a fresh one!

Which famous baseball player owns one of the largest sporting goods chain stores?

Albert G. Spalding, commonly known as Al Spalding. He founded the Spalding brand of sporting equipment.

Which US President had a very low opinion of the early versions of baseball?

Thomas Jefferson. He has been quoted as saying: "Games played with the ball and others of that nature, are too violent for the body and stamp no character on the mind".

Which is the only great-grandfather and great-grandson baseball player combination in Major League history?

Jim Bluejacket and Bill Wilkinson. Jim began his career in 1914 with the Boston Tip-Tops and retired in 1916. Bill began his career in 1985 with the Seattle Mariners and retired in 1988.

Lou Gehrig

What is the 'Chalmers Award' and to whom was it first given?

The Chalmers Award was the first 'Most Valuable Player' award established in baseball. It was presented between 1911 and 1914 by Chalmers Automotive. The first man to win it was Ty Cobb, who already owned a Chalmers automobile!

How did Baltimore Oriole's player Mark Smith injure his hand?

By sticking it in an air conditioner to "find out why it wasn't working"!

Which famous baseball legend has a disease named after him?

Lou Gehrig of the New York Yankees was diagnosed with a very rare disease called Amyotrophic Lateral Sclerosis, which causes spasms and paralysis and ended his professional baseball career. Since then, the disease was commonly known as Lou Gehrig's Disease.

Which Boston Red Sox player missed several games after injuring himself in a strange way?

Third baseman Wade Boggs. He strained his back while pulling on his cowboy boots!

FIFA

Are there any official football competitions for women?

Yes. The first FIFA Women's Football World Cup was held in 1991. In 1996, women's football was also made an Olympic event.

Is football an Olympic event?

Yes. Football was made an official Olympic event in 1900.

What is FIFA?

Short for Fédération Internationale de Football Association, FIFA is the world's highest controlling body for international football competitions.

What is the World Cup?

The World Cup is the most important international football competition in the world. It is organised by FIFA and is held every four years.

Where does the word 'soccer' come from?

When the London Football Association was formed, people started calling the ball-kicking game 'association football'. With time, 'association' became 'assoc' and finally, 'soccer'. However, in many countries of the world, the game is still known simply as 'football'.

FA Cup

When and where was the world's first football organisation formed?

On October 26, 1863, the London Football Association (FA) was formed in the Freemason's Tavern in London.

When were the rules of football officially written down for the first time?

On November 10, 1863, by the London Football Association. There were only 14 rules.

When was the first official international football competition held?

The first international football competition was held in 1872 between England and Scotland. It ended in a 0 - 0 draw.

When was modern English football invented?

In the 19th century, school children in England started playing a ball-kicking game similar to modern day football. It quickly became very popular and British sailors carried it to the rest of Europe, India and South America.

When was the first official football competition held?

The first official game, called the FA Cup, was played in 1871 in England. The Wanderers Club beat The Royal Engineers Club, 1 - 0.

24

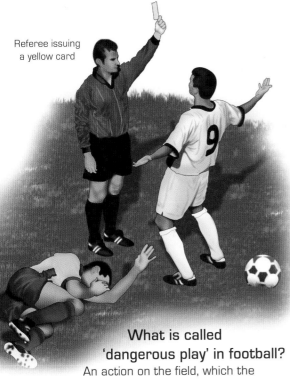

Referee issuing
a yellow card

What is the 'advantage rule'?

A referee can decide not to stop the game to award a foul, if allowing the game to continue creates an advantage for the fouled team.

How did the 'scorpion kick' originate?

During a 1995 match against Columbia, Colombian goalie Rene Higuita dived under the lobbed ball in mid-air to save the goal, by flicking his heels behind his head like a scorpion.

What is a 'bicycle kick'?

A kick where the player's body is horizontal in mid-air and the ball is struck over the player's head. This type of kick was popularised by football legend Pelé.

Football legend
Pele

What is called 'dangerous play' in football?

An action on the field, which the referee believes might have caused injury to other players, such as kicking the ball out of the goalie's hands. It is usually given a yellow card, but could also earn a red card as punishment.

What is a 'dropped ball'?

When the referee drops the ball between two opposing players. It indicates the continuation of the game when it has been interrupted for reasons other than a foul (for example, if a player is injured).

What must a player do to earn a 'cap'?

Play in a game as part of the national team. So, a player who has played in the national team 5 times, has been 'capped' 5 times, or has earned 5 'caps'.

Who was the 'Cruyff turn' named after?

Dutch International footballer Johann Cruyff created this turn in 1974 in his only World Cup match. The turn fools the opponent into thinking that the ball is being passed one way when it is actually being dragged in the opposite direction.

What does it mean to be 'booked' in a football match?

The term refers to a player's name being written down by the referee for actions meriting a yellow card or a red card.

In football language, what is a 'center'?

A pass that is kicked from the sides of the field into the opponent's penalty area.

In football, what is known as a 'chip'?

A high, arching shot that passes over the heads of defenders or the goalkeeper.

What is the Champions League?

Originally known as the European Cup, the Champions League is a tournament among those European clubs which finished at the top of their national leagues. It is organised by the Union of European Football Associations (UEFA).

Which is the richest football club on the planet?

Manchester United Football Club, in the English Premier League. It was the first club to reach an income of over £1 billion.

What is the Intercontinental Cup also known as?

The Toyota Cup. This is because the Toyota Company has been sponsoring this cup since 1980.

What is the competition among South American national football teams called?

The Copa America. It is one of the oldest international soccer tournaments, second only to the Olympics. It was held for the first time in 1916.

Which team has won the FA Cup the most number of times?

Manchester United. They have won the FA Cup 10 times!

Why do most fans consider the World Cup to be more important than the football event at the Olympics?

That's because the World Cup is a football-only sporting event. In the Olympics, football is only one of the many different games played.

What is the Confederations Cup?

Originally known as the King Fahd Cup, it is a competition among the continental champions of Africa, Asia, Europe, North America and South America. It was held for the first time in 1992. In 1997, FIFA renamed it the Confederations Cup. It is held on odd-numbered years.

What is the competition among African national football teams called?

The African Nations Cup. It began in 1957. It is held on every even-numbered year.

What is the Copa Libertadores?

It is a competition among South American football clubs (not national teams). It was established by the South American soccer confederation in 1960.

What is the CONCACAF Gold Cup?

It stands for the Confederation of North and Central American and Caribbean Football Gold Cup. It was held for the first time in 1963.

Copa America Cup

Who earned the highest transfer fee in soccer history?

France's Zinedine Zidane is reported to have earned the highest transfer fee of 13,033,000,000 Spanish Pesetas (£47 million), when he shifted from Juventus to Real Madrid on July 9, 2001.

Lizarazu, a Bayern Munich player

Zinedine Zidane, a Real Madrid player

Which team has won the Champions League the greatest number of times?

Real Madrid from Spain. They have played in the Champions League 12 times and have won it 9 times.

When was the first Champions League game played?

In 1956, when it was still known as the European Cup. Real Madrid from Spain won that year.

Which player is also known as 'Super Pippo'?

Filippo Inzaghi of the AC Milan Club in Italy. Super Pippo means 'super goof' in Italian!

Fillippo Inzaghi

What is the connection between Fabio Cannavaro and Diego Maradona?

Fabio Cannavaro of the Internazionale FC Club in Italy used to be Maradona's ball boy at the SSC Napoli Club!

When was the first ever FA Cup tournament held?

During 1871-1872, with only 15 participating clubs.

What is the UEFA Cup?

The Union of European Football Associations (UEFA) established this trophy for competition among those clubs which don't qualify for the Champions League. It was held for the first time in 1958.

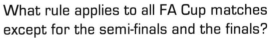

UEFA Cup

What rule applies to all FA Cup matches except for the semi-finals and the finals?

All matches, except for semi-finals and finals, if drawn after 90 minutes of play, are replayed on a different day. They do not go into overtime.

Which stadium has hosted the maximum number of FA Cup Finals?

Wembley Stadium. It hosted every single FA Cup Final from 1923 to 2000. That's 77 FA Cup Finals!

Which country won the first World Cup?

The first World Cup, held in 1930, was won by Uruguay.

Which was the most unlikely victory in football history?

The most unlikely victory happened during the 1984 European Championship final qualifier match. Spain needed a total of 11 goals to beat Malta and got them by scoring 9 goals during the second half of the match!

Why was the 1994 World Cup final special?

The 1994 World Cup final, played between Brazil and Italy, was the first ever World Cup final to be decided by penalty shoot-out. Brazil won 3-2.

For what is the England vs. Argentina game in the France 1998 World Cup remembered?

Due to the way in which England's midfielder David Beckham tackled Argentina's Diego Simeone, the referee showed Beckham the red card and sent him out of the game. Many believed that Beckham's un-sportsmanlike behaviour caused England to lose the match, as they were forced to play with only 10 players.

Which team has won the greatest number of consecutive games?

AC Milan, an Italian football club, holds the record for playing the most games without losing. They remained unbeaten for 58 games!

Which is the first-ever African nation to reach the World Cup quarter-finals?

Cameroon was the first African nation to reach the World Cup quarter-finals, during the 1990 World Cup.

Which team has scored the greatest number of goals in a single match?

According to FIFA records, it is the Australian team. Australia played against American Samoa in the World Cup qualifiers held in Coffs Harbour, Australia, in April 2001, beating Samoa 31-0!

Why is the phrase 'Hand of God' famous?

During the 1986 World Cup quarter finals, Argentina's Diego Maradona hit the ball into England's goal with his hand. This was technically a foul, but the referee, believing that Maradona had hit the ball with his head, awarded Argentina the goal! Since then, the goal has been referred to as the 'Hand of God' goal.

What made the 1934 World Cup game between Austria and France special?

During this game, the overtime rule was put to use for the first time. At the end of the normal 90 minutes, both teams were tied with 2 goals each.

Which team has scored the second largest number of goals in a single match?

The Australian team again! According to FIFA records, Australia beat Tonga 22-0 in Coffs Harbour, just two days before their victory over American Samoa!

Maradona

Pele

Who is considered to be the best football player the world has ever seen?

The Brazilian football player, Pelé. His real name is Edson Arantes do Nascimento. He led Brazil to 3 World Cup victories.

Who is Diego Armando Maradona?

Argentinean Diego Armando Maradona is regarded as one of the most talented players in football history. He led Argentina to victory in the Mexico 1986 World Cup.

Who is the oldest player ever to score a World Cup goal?

Roger Milla of Cameroon scored against Russia in the 1994 World Cup, at the age of 42.

Who is the world's highest earning football player?

England's team captain, David Robert Joseph Beckham is said to earn more than £10 million a year by means of wages and endorsements.

Who are some of the most admired players in football history?

Roger Milla of Cameroon; Paolo Rossi of Italy; Diego Maradona of Argentina; Pelé of Brazil; Franz Beckenbauer of Germany; and Michel Platini of France.

What made Davor Suker famous?

During France's 1998 World Cup, this Croatian player scored 6 goals, the highest by a player during that World Cup.

Gabriel Batistuta

Franz Beckenbauer

What makes German player Franz Beckenbauer special?

He was the first person to win the World Cup both as a captain (1974) and as a team manager (1990).

What made Argentinean player Gabriel Batistuta famous?

He was the first player to score a hat trick (scoring 3 goals one after the other) in 2 consecutive World Cup finals.

What makes German players Fritz Walter and Otmar Walter special?

They were the first pair of brothers to play on the winning team in a World Cup final, in the Switzerland 1954 World Cup.

How much did Michael Owen earn as a Youth Training Scheme (YTS) trainee?

Michael Owen earned £42.50 a week during his National Vocational Qualification (NVQ) in Leisure Management. He began playing professional football at 17 and now earns millions of pounds.

29

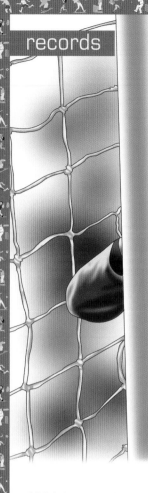

Dino Zoff

Who is the oldest player to have played in a World Cup final?
Italian goalkeeper Dino Zoff was 40 years and 133 days old when he played in the Spain 1982 World Cup.

Who is the youngest footballer to have played in a World Cup final?
Brazilian legend Pelé. When he played in the Sweden 1958 World Cup, he was 17 years and 249 days old.

Which goalkeeper successfully defended his goal for the longest time?
During the Italy 1990 World Cup, Italian goalie Walter Zenga successfully defended his goal for 517 minutes (approximately 8.5 hours!).

Who were the first father and son to play in World Cup matches?
Martin and Jose Vontrola. Martin played in the Italy 1934 World Cup. His son Jose played in the Mexico 1970 World Cup.

Which team has scored the most goals in a single World Cup?
Hungary. They scored a total of 27 goals during the Switzerland 1954 World Cup.

Who scored the fastest goal in World Cup finals history?
Hakan Sükür of Turkey scored his first goal 11 seconds after the start of the game against the Korean Republic in the 2002 FIFA World Cup.

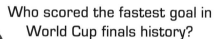

Hakan Sukur

What is the biggest margin by which a team has won a World Cup match?
In Hungary's win over El Salvador in the Spain 1982 World Cup, Hungary won 10-1!

Who has coached the largest number of teams in the World Cup?
Bora Milutinovic of Yugoslavia. He coached Mexico in 1986, Costa Rica in 1990, USA in 1994, Nigeria in 1998 and China in 2002.

Bora Milutinovic

Which was the first team to win two consecutive World Cups?
Italy won the World Cup in 1934 and then again in 1938.

Who is the youngest coach to have taken a team to the World Cup?
Juan Jose Tramutola of Argentina. When he took the Argentinean team to the Uruguay 1930 World Cup, he was 27 years and 267 days old.

What made the inauguration of the Daegu Main Stadium in Korea special?

It was inaugurated with a game between the Santos team (Brazil) and the Ilwha team (Seongnam). Almost 70,000 tickets were distributed nation-wide, free of charge!

Which is the world's largest stadium?

The Maracana Stadium in Rio de Janeiro, Brazil. It can seat 125,000 people.

What is special about the Kashima Soccer Stadium in Ibaraki, Japan?

Standing at the gate of the stadium is a statue of Ibaraki's favourite footballer: Brazilian football star Zico.

Which is the biggest football stadium in Europe?

The Nou Camp stadium in Barcelona, Spain. It is capable of seating 98,000 people.

What is unique about the Jeonju World Cup Stadium?

The Jeonju World Cup Stadium in Korea has 4 concave roofs, hanging from suspension cables. They are built in the shape of a fan, representing the strings of a Gaya harp, a traditional Korean musical instrument.

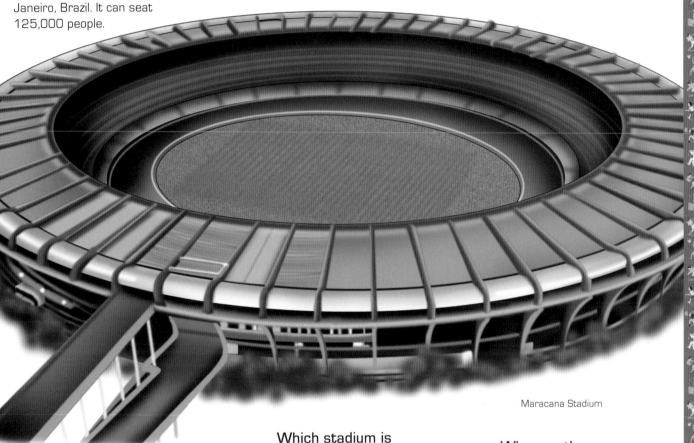

Maracana Stadium

Where can you find the famous 'Red Café'?

In the Old Trafford Stadium in Manchester, England. After a match, fans can go there to chat with the players.

Which stadium's football pitch is located on top of a four-storey parking lot?

The Louis II Stadium in Monte Carlo, Monaco, built in 1939, rests on top of a carpark.

Which stadium is nicknamed the 'Scala' of football?

The San Siro Stadium in Milan, Italy. It is one of the few stadiums in the world built only for football.

What is the Stadio Olimpico in Rome, Italy famous for?

The entire stadium is covered with a transparent roof! It was added specially for the 1990 World Cup.

Why was the Santiago Bernabeu Stadium built?

To replace the Chamartin Stadium, which was the home stadium of the Real Madrid football club, until it was destroyed during the Spanish civil war. The club's president, Mr. Santiago Bernabeu, had a new stadium built in its place and named it after himself.

Senegal team
players

Which famous England football player of the past was one of FIFA's Ambassadors for the 2002 World Cup?
Sir Bobby Charlton, a member of the 1966 team that won the only World Cup for England.

Sir Bobby
Charlton

What is the Senegal team's footballing nickname?
The Lions of Tarenga.

Which country considered putting a picture of a football on their national flag?
In the early 70's, the Brazilian government almost passed a law to change the globe on the Brazilian flag into a football!

Who scored the first goal in the history of the World Cup?
Laurent of France, on July 13, 1930, in the game between France and Mexico.

When was the referee's whistle first introduced into football?
In 1878. Before that, referees had to wave a handkerchief!

When was player substitution in professional football allowed for the first time?
In 1970, 40 years after the first World Cup!

Which team holds the English record for the longest-ever free kick?
The Chelsea team. Their free kick went out of the ground and landed on a freight train. The ball was recovered a few miles down the track!

A free kick
by a Chelsea
player

Who was the first coach to be fired during a World Cup?
Carlos Alberto Parreira, the coach for the Saudi Arabian team, was sacked after the team lost their first 2 games in the 1998 World Cup.

What did Japanese fans do in the France 1998 World Cup, that other fans did not?
Japanese fans stayed behind after the match was over to clean up after themselves!

Which famous football player composed the soundtrack for a movie?
In 1977, Brazilian football legend Pelé composed the soundtrack for a movie about his life.

FIFA
World
Cup
Trophy

What was special about Ronaldo's World Cup 2002 record?

In the World Cup 2002 matches, Brazil's Ronaldo scored 5 goals by himself, as many as those scored by the entire England team.

Ronaldo

What is the current FIFA World Cup trophy?

The current trophy was created in 1971. It depicts two players holding a globe in their raised hands. Designed by Italian Silvio Gazzanigi and made for $50,000 out of 18-carat gold, it is now valued at over $10,000,000!

What happened to the 1966 World Cup trophy?

The Jules Rimet trophy was stolen at an exhibition in March and FIFA had planned to stage the World Cup without it. Thankfully, a dog named Pickles found it wrapped up in a newspaper in some bushes in South London, just a week after the theft!

Which ritual is believed to be behind France's success in the 1998 World Cup?

Some attributed the team's success to defender Laurent Blanc's kiss on goalkeeper Fabien Barthez's bald head before each game!

When was a mascot first used to promote the World Cup?

During the England 1966 World Cup. The mascot was a cartoon of a football-playing lion called 'World Cup Willie'. Since then, every World Cup has had its own mascot.

Which football club was sponsored by a music band?

In the early 90's, Scottish football club Clydebank was sponsored by a music band called Wet Wet Wet!

2002 FIFA Mascots

Which game started with one of the teams having only 10 players, instead of the usual 11 and why?

During the Brazil 1950 World Cup, Yugoslavian player Rajko Mitic hit his head on a metal pipe while running out onto the field, knocking himself unconscious. Since player substitutions weren't allowed until 1970, Yugoslavia had to play with only 10 players! Brazil won 5 - 0.

Who scored the fastest hat trick in the history of football?

Japanese player Masashi Nakayama. During an official match against Brunei in 2000, he scored 3 goals in the first 3 minutes and 15 seconds of the game!

Does David Beckham wear the same pair of shoes in every match?

David Beckham wears a new custom-made pair of football boots in every game that he plays. His shoes are said to cost £300 a pair! He wears a pair again only if he feels he scored a very good goal wearing them.

Which famous football player was named Athlete of the 20th Century and was also given the International Peace Award?

Brazil's football legend, Pelé. He was named Athlete of the Century in 1980 and is the only professional athlete to have been honoured with the International Peace Award, which he received in 1978.

When was the first Grand Prix held?

The French Grand Prix at Le Mans in 1906, was the world's first race to be given the title of Grand Prix. The winner drove a Renault at 101.39 kilometres per hour (63 mph) to win the 1,126.54 kilometres (700 miles) long race.

When was the Formula One World Championship born?

The first Formula One World Championship was held on May 13, 1950, at the Silverstone circuit in the UK. The spectators of the race were members of the British royal family.

Which Grand Prix event was also the first 'International Formula One Race'?

The Pau Grand Prix held on April 10, 1950 was the first International Formula One Race. Juan Manuel Fangio, driving a Maserati, won the race.

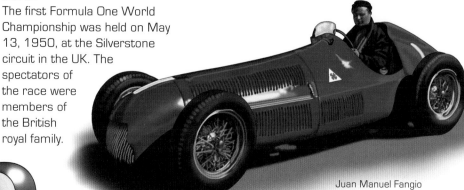

Juan Manuel Fangio

Which invention in the 1920s changed the face of car racing?

Rear-view mirrors were invented in the 1920s. Before this invention, a mechanic seated in the car performed the task of warning the driver that someone was trying to overtake him.

Why were shallow pits dug along the early racetracks?

Early racing cars had tyres that could be easily removed from the rim. Mechanics would sit in the pits and repair the damaged tyres during the race.

What was Formula A, introduced in 1950?

Formula One was first known as Formula A and it ruled that all Grand Prix races had to cover a minimum distance of 300 kilometres (186 miles). The earlier races used to run into many days and covered no less than 500 kilometres (311 miles).

When did advertisements first appear on Formula One cars during a championship?

It was in 1968 that advertisements were first seen on F1 cars. The first advertisement was that for Gold Leaf cigarettes, displayed on the car of British driver, Colin Chapman.

Were Grand Prix events held in Europe during World War I?

No. Grand Prix events were not held during the World War years.

When did pits first appear along racetracks?

The 1908 race at Targa Florio, Italy first saw the appearance of pits along the racetrack.

When did single-seater cars first appear?

Single-seater cars appeared only in the late 1920s. Cars were divided into groups on the basis of the kind of engine (petrol or steam) they ran on and on the number of seats they had.

Single Seater Racing Cars

Who organizes the F1 championships?

The Federation Internationale de l'Automobile (FIA), set up in 1946, organises motor sport events, such as Formula One and World Rally championships. It also makes the rules for these races.

What are Formula One regulations?

The FIA draws up rules about the dimensions of the car, the kind of fuel to be used and the nature of the engine. All Formula One cars must follow these regulations.

Do the rules for Formula One races differ from one circuit to another?

The FIA draws common rules for Formula One races taking place at Grand Prix circuits all over the world. The rules do not differ from circuit to circuit.

On what basis are the Formula One regulations drawn?

The Formula One regulations are drawn keeping in mind the safety of the drivers, without taking away speed and excitement from the race.

How many Grand Prix events must be held for a world championship?

The Formula One World Championship must include a minimum of eight and a maximum of seventeen Grand Prix events.

How were car races organised before the FIA was set up in 1946?

Automobile clubs organised car races. The Association Internationale des Automobiles Clubs Reconnus (AIACR) was formed in 1904 to take automobile racing to the international level. The AIACR was reformed in 1946 and renamed as the Federation Internationale de l' Automobile (FIA).

Is Grand Prix the same as Formula One?

Grand Prix races lead to the Formula One World Championship. Any racing event that is not a part of the world championship cannot be called Grand Prix. The Grand Prix de Pau, which is a Formula 3000 event, is an exception.

Who are Car Stewards?

Car Stewards are the three referees who see to it that all participating cars follow the Formula One regulations. At least one of them does not belong to the country where the race is being held.

Do all Grand Prix events have the same timetable?

All Grand Prix events follow the same timetable. They are held over weekends, from Friday to Sunday and have fixed timings allotted for practice sessions. One practice session at the Monaco Grand Prix is held on Thursday.

What is the punishment given to a driver who breaks the rules?

The punishment meted out to a driver who breaks the rules may range from a cash fine to being disqualified from the championship. Where the driver *is* allowed to take part in the race, he may be asked to start a few seconds after the other participants.

What does the yellow flag indicate?

Overtaking under the yellow flag is not allowed. The yellow flag, if kept stationary, conveys a warning to the drivers not to overtake. If waved, the yellow flag issues an order for them to slow down.

Is there a speed limit to be observed during a Grand Prix?

The drivers must observe a speed limit of 80 to 120 kilometres per hour (49.71-74.56 mph) in the pit lane, before they reach the starting grid. Each car has a 'speed limiter' that, if activated by the driver, does not allow the car to exceed the speed limit.

Are the drivers allowed to practise on the track before the race?

Practice sessions are conducted a day before the Grand Prix event. A half-an-hour long warm-up round takes place four and a half hours before the race, so that the drivers get used to the conditions on the racetrack.

What happens if it begins to rain after the warm up?

If it begins to rain after the warm up but before the race begins, an additional 15-minute practice session is announced so that the drivers adapt themselves to the weather.

How long does a Grand Prix last?

A Grand Prix lasts for no more than two hours. The distance covered by the drivers during the race must not exceed 305 kilometres (189.52 miles).

Which signal indicates the start of a race?

Once all cars have taken their position, the starting procedure begins. Five lights turn red one after the other until all the five are lit. They are then put out simultaneously. This is the signal for the race to begin.

How many flags are used as signals in Grand Prix events?

There are in all nine flags that represent nine different signals, which may be used during a Grand Prix event. These flags vary not just in their colour, but also in the design printed on them.

Is a Grand Prix postponed in the event of rain?

A Grand Prix is not normally held up because of rain. Formula One cars are equipped with a red light in the rear. The light is switched on when it rains in order to avoid car collisions.

Is it possible to catch a driver who jumps the start signal?

Each position on the starting grid has sensors that catch the cars' movements. A driver who tries to begin before the five lights are put out, is given a punishment by the authorities.

What do the drivers do if they run out of fuel during the race?

The drivers are allowed to refuel their cars during the race, but refuelling must be carried out only with the equipment specified by the FIA.

Re-fuelling a car during a race

Whose brother is a record-breaking F1 champion?
F1 driver Ralf Schumacher. His elder brother, Michael Schumacher, is a 4 times world champion.

Ralf Schumacher

Can any driver participate in a Grand Prix?
A driver can compete in a Grand Prix only if he holds a 'super licence,' for which he is eligible on the basis of his past records in junior level races. Competing drivers must have a contract with a team scheduled to participate in the Grand Prix.

Who was the highlight of the 1928 Targa Florio race?
Elizabeth Junek. On one of the world's most difficult tracks, she raced past the champions of the era. The race was finally won by Albert Divo.

Who was a karting and sports car racing veteran before getting into Formula One Racing?
The Brazilian driver, Nelson Piquet. He had three championship wins during his 13-year-long Formula One career.

Who was a F1 driver and an industrial engineer as well as an author?
Piero Taruffi was an F1 champion and a qualified engineer as well as an author. He wrote the book, 'The Technique of Motor Racing,' which was published in 1959.

How old was Michael Schumacher when he first took part in a kart race?
He was five when he first participated in a kart race. His father, Rolf, built his first kart.

For which British driver did an appendix operation prove fatal?
Reg Parnell, an F1 driver and a team manager, passed away after a seemingly normal appendix operation.

Michael Schumacher

What connects Barbara Cartland to car racing?
This novelist was a patron of a women's racing group in England in the 1920s.

Which F1 driver, also a pilot, became a secret agent during World War II?
British driver George Abecassis served the Royal Air Force during World War II as part of the secret Moon squadron. His job was to ferry British secret agents in and out of France in a Lysander aircraft.

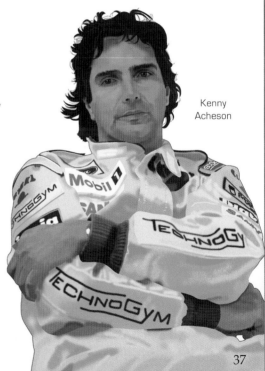

Kenny Acheson

On what condition was Kenny Acheson allowed to participate in his first car race?
Kenny Acheson, son of a Formula Ford driver, was allowed by his father to take part in a Formula Ford race on the condition that he quit smoking. Kenny went on to win three Formula Ford championship titles.

37

cars and constructors

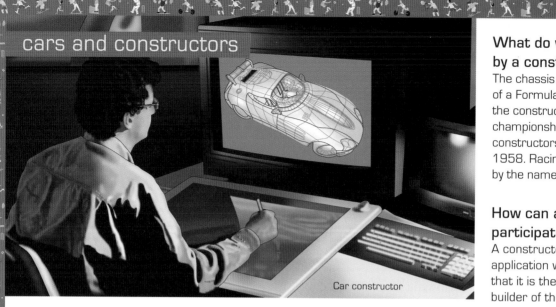

Car constructor

What do we mean by a constructor?

The chassis (framework) builder of a Formula One car is called the constructor. The F1 world championship title for the constructors was introduced in 1958. Racing teams are known by the names of their constructors.

How can a constructor participate in a Grand Prix?

A constructor must submit an application with the FIA, stating that it is the designer and builder of the chassis of its car.

Who was knighted in 1968 for his work in the automotive industry?

David Brown was knighted in 1968 for his work in the automotive industry. Brown took over the Aston Martin Lagonda Limited in the late 1940s.

Which F1 car, first raced in 1970, featured a cloaked man on its team badge?

The Shadow, designed by Trevor Harris. It was discovered to be an unreliable car after its first race.

What kind of car did Team Lotus introduce to Formula One in 1963?

Team Lotus introduced a car with a single-piece chassis in 1963. The car, Lotus 25, designed by Colin Chapman and driven by Jimmy Clark, won the team its first Formula One Drivers' World Championship.

Which was Britain's top constructor in the 1950s?

Hersham and Walton Motors, founded by F1 drivers, George Abecassis and John Heath. It was known for its 1949 car, which could be raced either as a sports car or a single-seater.

When was a rear-engine first used in F1 cars?

The 1959-60 Cooper team was the first to use cars with rear-engines. Sir Jack Brabham won two championships, one after another, when he first drove these cars.

What is the Thoroughbred Grand Prix Car Championship?

Organized by the FIA, it is a racing event for second-hand F1 cars built between 1966 and 1985. It is compulsory for these cars to have competed in at least one international F1 event in their heyday.

Which constructor manufactures the chassis as well as car engines?

Currently the most successful constructor, Ferrari, manufactures the chassis as well as the engines of its F1 cars. No other constructor manufactures car engines.

Ferrari

Aston Martin

Which racing car was built by Robert Bamford and Lionel Martin in 1913 in their garage in Kensington?

They built the Aston Martin in their garage, when they fitted the engine of one car in to the chassis of another. It became an active racing car in the 1950s.

38

tech talk

How did Bridgestone Tyres get its name?
Two Japanese men, Shojiro and Tokoshiro Ishibashi, owned the company. Their surname when divided and translated into English means 'stone' (Ishi) and 'bridge' (Bashi). They joined the two words and named the company, Bridgestone.

What is aerodynamics?
The most important aspect of car design, aerodynamics is the study of the forces of resistance and pressure that are created due to the flow of air around, under or above a moving car.

Why is the rear wing of a racing car important?
The rear wing helps to keep the car's rear wheels firmly on the racetrack.

What is special about Ferrari's F1 2000 engine?
The Ferrari F1 2000 with a V10 engine was a smaller, more compact and more powerful version of the typical Ferrari engine. Michael Schumacher drove it to victory in October 2000.

How long does it take to change tyres during a race?
Experienced teams usually take 5 to 10 seconds to change all four tyres and refuel the car during a race. Tyres made from soft rubber need to be changed more often.

How much air pressure do Formula One cars usually have?
A Formula One car is said to have enough aerodynamic downforce (the pressure of air on a car as it races) to drive upside down at over 100 kilometres (62.13 miles) per hour!

What are the functions of steering wheels in F1 cars?
Apart from its basic steering function, the steering wheel also regulates the gear-change, clutch, engine, radio, digital alarms and toggle switch functions.

What is the maximum number of tyres that a driver may use during a Grand Prix?
A driver may use a maximum of 28 tyres (14 each for front and rear) for the practice rounds, as well as the final race.

Who started the Goodyear Tyre Company in 1898?
Frank and Charles Seiberling started a tyre company in 1898, naming it after Charles Goodyear. Goodyear Tyres is the biggest producer of tyres and rubber. It also began building airships (zeppelins) in 1924.

How many gears are there in a Formula One car's gearbox?
On average a Formula One gearbox consists of 6-7 gears that change automatically in less than one second. The 575M Maranello was the first 12-cylinder Ferrari to be fitted with an F1-type gearbox.

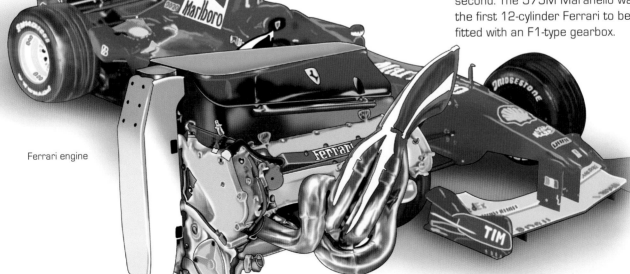
Ferrari engine

39

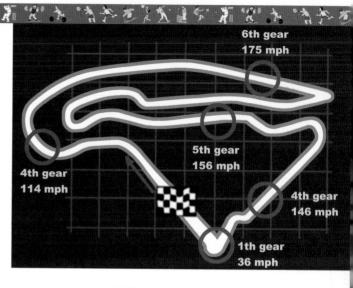

6th gear
175 mph

5th gear
156 mph

4th gear
114 mph

4th gear
146 mph

1th gear
36 mph

Can any circuit (racetrack) be used for Grand Prix events?

In its early years a Grand Prix could be held anywhere, but now the FIA is very strict about the circuits used. A circuit must meet the size, safety and other conditions drawn by the FIA.

Where was the first major Grand Prix held?

The Grand Prix de l'Automobile Club de France, the first big-circuit race, was held at Le Mans, France in 1906. The race went on for two days.

What is special about the Circuit de Catalunya in Barcelona, Spain?

The Circuit de Catalunya in Barcelona which was opened in 1991 has three different courses - the Grand Prix Circuit, the National Circuit and the School Circuit that measure 4.73 km, 3.07 km and 1.70 km respectively.

What is special about Nurburgring, Germany?

Nurburgring has a leisure park with amusement games, a museum displaying old F1 cars and a hotel complex. It was used for F1 races in 1950 and was then closed down for almost ten years. It reopened after renovation in 1984.

What was the Suzuka Circuit in Japan originally used for?

It was originally part of a motorcycle theme park. Situated close to the Honda factory, it exhibited cars as well. It hosted the first Japanese Grand Prix in 1963.

Why do Grand Prix circuits have sharp bends?

Formula One cars can reach speeds as high as 350 kilometres per hour (217.48 mph) on a straight path. Bends are introduced in order to prevent excessive speeds that may lead to dangerous accidents and, of course, to test the drivers' skills.

Which F1 circuit was built as a military training base for bomber aircraft?

The Sebring International Raceway in the US was built in 1941 as Hendrick's Field, a training base for bomber aircraft. It was first used as a racetrack in 1950 and as a Formula One circuit in 1959.

Which is the longest circuit in the world?

The Spa Francorchamps in Belgium. It measures 6.96 kilometres (4.32 miles) in length and includes part of a public road, cutting through the Ardennes Forest.

Why is the Monaco circuit called the slowest circuit in the world?

It is called the slowest circuit in the world because F1 drivers cannot reach a high speed on it. They are forced to slow down as they avoid pavements and manhole covers on the streets. The Monza in Italy is the world's fastest circuit.

Which Grand Prix circuit consists entirely of city streets?

The Monaco circuit. It is the shortest circuit in the world, with a length of 3.33 kilometres (2.07 miles).

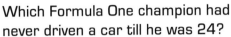

Which F1 driver has had the maximum Grand Prix wins in his native country?

The French driver Alain Prost won six French Grand Prix events - the highest number of Grand Prix wins by a driver in his native country.

Who is Ferrari's most successful driver ever?

Michael Schumacher, Ferrari's most successful driver, has won the maximum number of Grand Prix events in history.

Which Formula One champion had never driven a car till he was 24?

Graham Hill. He won 5 consecutive Grand Prix titles at Monaco and is the only driver to have won the Indianapolis, Le Mans and F1 World Championships.

Who has the maximum F1 world championships to his name?

Michael Schumacher. He equalled Juan Manuel Fangio's record of winning the F1 World Championship five times, at the French Grand Prix in 2002. Fangio did so between 1951 and 1957, driving for four different teams (Alfa Romeo, Mercedes, Ferrari and Maserati).

Alain Prost

Who is the oldest Formula One World Champion?

The oldest ever Formula One world champion is Argentina's Juan Manuel Fangio, who won his last World Championship in Monaco on August 4, 1957, aged 46 years.

Who is the only Formula One driver to have won a world title in a car of his own construction?

Sir Jack Brabham who was knighted for his achievements in motor sport, became the only driver in history to have won a world title in a car of his own construction when he drove the BT19 to victory in 1966.

Which F1 champion's father had been a world champion too?

Damon Hill, a former motorcycle racer and the 1996 F1 World Champion, is the son of Graham Hill, a world champion from the 1960s.

After how many years of Formula One Racing did Nigel Mansell win his first world championship?

Nigel Mansell had raced for 12 years before he won his first World Championship in 1992.

Ayrton Senna

Nigel Mansell

Who broke Graham Hill's record of winning 5 Monaco Grand Prix titles?

The Brazilian racing great, Ayrton Senna, broke the record when he won the 6th consecutive Grand Prix at Monaco in 1993.

Who was the youngest ever driver to take part in a Grand Prix?

Mike Thackwell became the youngest ever Grand Prix driver when he took part in the Canadian Grand Prix in 1980 at the age of 19 years.

Who was the first woman F1 driver?

Maria Teresa de Filippis was the first woman F1 driver. She stood tenth in her first Grand Prix at Belgium in 1958.

Which was the first venue to host the French Grand Prix?

The first French Grand Prix was held at Reims in 1950. Seven different circuits have hosted the French Grand Prix since then.

Jim Clark

Who was the first Briton to win the Indianapolis 500 race?

Jim Clark, the 1963 and 1965 world champion, was the first driver from England to win the Indianapolis 500 race.

Which F1 driver is one of the top ten wealthiest athletes of the world?

Michael Schumacher, the first motor racing star to be one of the top ten wealthiest athletes, earns an annual income of US $31 million from Ferrari.

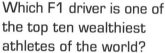

John Surtees

Where was the first Las Vegas Grand Prix in 1981 held?

The first Las Vegas Grand Prix, also called the Caesars Palace Grand Prix, was held in the car park of the Caesars Palace Casino, Las Vegas.

Who was the first F1 world champion?

Giuseppe Farina, driving an Alfa Romeo, won the first Formula One Grand Prix held at the Silverstone circuit, UK in 1950.

Where was the first South American round in the F1 world championship held?

It was held at the Buenos Aires Circuit, Argentina, in 1953. The venue was not big enough to hold all the spectators. Many sat at the edge of the racetrack and nine were killed in a car crash.

Which driver won Formula One world titles in car as well as motorbike racing?

John Surtees was the first (and the only) driver to win F1 world championships in both motorbike and car racing. Seven times world champion in motorbike racing, Surtees was called 'Wire of the Wind' and 'Big John'.

When did Ferrari first win a world championship event?

Ferrari had its first-ever F1 victory when its driver Froilan Gonzalez won the R.A.C. British Grand Prix at Silverstone in 1951.

Who won the first Grand Prix that he participated in?

Giancarlo Baghetti became the only driver to have won his debut Grand Prix, when he stood first in his debut race at Reims, France in 1961.

1951 Ferrari

Why was motor racing banned in Switzerland?

Motor racing was banned in Switzerland, after Pierre Levegh's Mercedes Benz sports car crashed into the Le Mans grand stand killing 81 spectators and injuring hundreds of others, in 1955.

When are safety cars used during a race?

They are used when there is an accident at the circuit, or in case the lives of the participating drivers are in danger.

Which driver was killed when his car hit some trees on a rainy day?

Jim Clark, one of the best drivers of the 1960s, was killed when his car hit some fir trees at a speed of 240 kilometres per hour (149.13 mph), on a rainy day at Hockenheim, Germany, in 1968.

Which F1 champion retired from the game after a car crash in 1962?

Sir Stirling Moss decided to hang up his boots for good after his car crashed head-on into an earth bank at a non-championship race meeting at Goodwood, in 1962.

What made Jackie Stewart take up the cause of safety on F1 circuits?

Jackie Stewart was trapped in his car after a crash at the Spa Francorchamps, Belgium, in 1966. This crash led him to campaign actively for safety in motor racing.

Which was the shortest race in the history of F1?

The 1991 Australian Grand Prix in Adelaide was halted after just 14 laps due to very heavy rainfall, making it the shortest ever F1 race. Heavy rainfall increases the possibility of car crashes at the circuit.

Safety Car

Do the helmets of Formula One drivers break?

In most accidents, the helmets worn by the drivers stay intact. They are made of strong bullet-proof material.

What does a SC board along with a yellow flag signify?

It means that the race has been halted and that all cars must reduce their speed and line up behind the safety car.

What does a red 'E' on a 10-centimetre white circle indicate?

It indicates the fire-extinguisher system installed in the cockpit and the engine of F1 cars. The driver in the cockpit or the marshals outside the car can activate the extinguisher.

What happened during the Australian Grand Prix in 2001?

A wheel flew loose from Jacques Villeneuve's BAR and collided with Ralf Schumacher's Williams. The loose wheel hit a track marshal, who died on the spot. Many spectators were also injured.

43